BIBLE CHRISTIANITY VERSUS ROMAN CATHOLIC SYSTEM

*The Roman Catholic System Hates
the King James Bible*

Alejandro Amores

ISBN 979-8-89485-013-9 (Paperback)
ISBN 979-8-89485-014-6 (Digital)

Covenant Books
11661 Hwy 707
Murrells Inlet, SC 29576
www.covenantbooks.com

Dedicated to our God and Lord Jesus Christ, who makes all things possible through the Holy Spirit.
Life verse: Joshua 24:15

Thy word is true from the beginning.
—Psalm 119:160

For you have perverted the words of the Living
God or the Lord of hosts our God.
—Jeremiah 23:36

CONTENTS

PREFACE

Members of the Roman Catholic system are counted in the hundreds of millions—some say a billion plus—and there are two requirements for being a Roman Catholic.

First, if you are born in a country where the official religion is the Roman Catholic system, then you are perceived as a Roman Catholic.

Second, if you are born in such a country, it is expected at the very least to get baptized as such, and therefore, your religion is listed as the Roman Catholic system on the birth certificate. Only the most devout will go on to follow their practices, traditions, and doctrines. In my personal witness, I have been told I was born a Roman Catholic and I'll die a Roman Catholic. My parents were Roman Catholic. I'll die a Roman Catholic. This is encouraged by the Roman Catholic system, which says that the church is salvation. Roman Catholics are encouraged to follow the seven sacraments that lead to salvation; nowhere is it encouraged to attend church except in observance of such sacraments. True Bible Christians differ from this process, as it requires an individual decision whenever a person is capable of understanding from the word of God what true salvation is. The Bible clearly states that a person must be born again to receive the gift of salvation, taking the step described in the Gospel of John 3:3.

The purpose of this writing is to clearly define the differences between the Roman Catholic system and true Bible Christianity. It is necessary to detail some of the doctrines of the Roman Catholic system that have caused so much damage to the work of Christ. The Roman Catholic system is what's portrayed to the world as the Church of Christ; nothing could be further from the truth once we find out about the reality.

The Bible tells us the story of two men who were crucified along with Christ, one on either side. Of the two men, one recognized Christ as the Lord and humbly asked that Christ would remember him. Jesus, in reply, promised this one that that very day, when he would die, he would go to paradise; salvation was achieved—no church membership, no sacraments, only the simple recognition of who Christ was—at which time that person became born again and was on his way to heaven based on the promise of Christ.

If you understand the principles of biblical Christianity and compare it with all other religions, you will be able to distinguish between "the way" (Acts 9:2) and all other ways. And the reason I use the Roman Catholic system in comparison is to try to dispel the fallacy that when the world says Christian, it should not default to the Roman Catholic system, being that in the Judeo-Christian western world system, we live in Christianity, which is prevalent, but we must establish a relationship between real Christianity and other so-called Christians.

INTRODUCTION

Translation: It is that which opens the window to let in the light; that which breaks the shell so that we may eat the kernel; that which puts aside the curtain so that we may look into the most holy place; that which removes the cover of the well so that we may come by the water.

CHAPTER 1

Confusion
Why Is the Roman Catholic System Confused with Bible Christianity

It started with Emperor Constantine seeing a vision in the sky, and he was instructed to follow the vision to victory over his rival, thereby securing his rule as sole emperor of the Roman Empire. It is accepted that Constantine converted to Christianity as a result. He legalized Christianity after centuries of persecution and extermination.

Constantine embarked on a mission to legitimize Christianity, but on his terms, followers of Christ chose to compromise in order to fit in with this newfound acceptance. Others, true Bible-believing Christians, refused to blend in and instead continued in their brand of Christianity passed down by the apostles and the early church fathers according to the teachings of Christ. Up to this time, Bible-believing Christians had spread throughout the whole world as commanded by Jesus. These Bible-believing Christians had the Old Testament scriptures, gospels, and early Christian writings, which later became the basis for the Bible we have today. The Hebrews had kept their writings in the Hebrew language, and the newer writings had been done in the Greek language, which was the predominant language of the world at the time. These scriptures had been translated into local languages, and people heard the word preached in their native tongues. Even before such translations had been made,

God made sure that the preached word would be heard by people in their own language (Acts chapter 2, King James Bible).

These early scriptures had been copied and distributed throughout the Roman Empire wherever you would find churches that had been established. Sometimes it would be a page or two, or it would be a whole chapter and maybe even a whole book. Paul the apostle, after his conversion from being a persecutor of Christianity, became a preacher of Christianity and established his base of operations at a church in Syria in a town called Antioch. This church in Antioch, where Christians were first called Christians (Acts chapter 11), put together a book of scriptures in the Syriac language called the Peshitta Bible around the year AD 150. This Bible is still in use today in some churches in that area.

In the second century AD, we found in the region of Northern Italy a Bible called the Italic Bible. We also found another early Bible among the Gothic tribes of Europe. These Bibles contained the available works as copied from the originals; these copies had been carefully made, as was the tradition passed down by the Hebrews of meticulously copying down the word of God.

When Constantine legalized Christianity on his own terms, he came up with the Bible that would be used throughout the empire. He commissioned Eusebius (early fourth century AD) of Jerusalem to make a translation from the available material at the time. Later in the same century, Jerome would translate Eusebius's work into the Latin language and produce fifty copies to be distributed throughout the Roman Empire. This would be the official Bible of Constantine's Christianity. Deviations from this Bible would not be tolerated, and copies of any other works would be hunted down and burned. Jerome's Bible was called the Latin Vulgate. Prior to the time when Constantine became emperor of the Roman Empire, it was customary to worship these emperors as gods. Not much changed when Constantine became emperor; this custom continued through Constantine and subsequent emperors.

Only a short five hundred years later, Charlemagne, the ruler of Europe, was named the emperor of the Holy Roman Empire by a pope. You can see the blurring and the mingling of church and state already taking place by this time. The pope issue had not been addressed earlier; however, when Constantine became emperor, making Christianity the religion of the empire and therefore its first ruler, people debated whether he was in fact the first pope. Definition of the pope being the head of the church. Here's where the Roman Catholic system has a problem of tracing back from their first pope to the current pope: we find no such system in Bible Christianity.

What happened between the time of Constantine and Charlamagne is very important. Instead of preaching the gospel of Jesus Christ, the Roman Empire continued to propagate Constantine's brand of Christianity, mixing the pagan with the gospel of Christ in order to accommodate its far-flung empire's many different religions. Constantine would force conversion to his Christianity on his subjects and would force his Bible on the empire. This was indeed the beginning of what we have come to know as the Dark Ages.

Christ's light to the world was being put out by this new system. During these dark ages, if this new system was not accepted as their brand of Christianity, the subjects were persecuted, suppressed, killed, or exiled. This was the beginning of the Roman Catholic system, rife with abuse from then until the present time. This system has its present-day headquarters in the Vatican City, which is an independent state within the city of Rome in the country of Italy. It is one of the richest, if not the richest, institutions on the face of the earth. It will take a separate book to detail how this was accomplished, but don't forget it had its start as the Roman Empire. This Roman Catholic system is a political system as well as a religious system. The warning of Paul the apostle in 2 Timothy, chapter 3, about perilous times to come had arrived.

CHAPTER 2

Persecution
2 Peter 2:1

The Roman Catholic system claims the Apostle Peter as the first pope. When Constantine became the first Christian emperor, he never titled himself as a pope, nor was there a pope mentioned in the Christian church in the time of Constantine. This is totally made up by the Roman Catholic system. This was a time of superstition, paganism, and many other religions. When Constantine became Christian, all these beliefs were mingled into it. The Apostle Peter warned in 2 Peter 2:1 about this. Shortly after the transformation of the Roman Empire, the warning of Peter came true. The new system embarked on a long list of false doctrines. They persecuted Bibles that differed from Jerome's Bible; any other Bible would be collected and burned. Considering that only fifty Bibles were in existence during the Roman Empire and that these were not available to the regular public, it's no wonder this period has come to be known as the start of the Dark Ages.

The Roman Empire forcibly converted all those pagans to Constantine's Christianity under the threat of converting them or suffering the consequences. Converting people forcibly is not exactly what Jesus had in mind when he explained to Nicodemus in the Gospel of John, chapter 3, that he needed to be born again, and specifically in John 3:16 that a person needs to believe in Jesus to receive eternal life. Constantine's Christianity continued to introduce changes, starting with making Latin the language of the Word of God, setting up holy sites, and setting up a system of sainthood—this practice is in direct contradiction to what the Bible calls saints. We see references to saints in the letter to the Hebrews, chapter 11, normally called the Hall of Faith, where we see believers in God through the ages, also references made to believers as saints throughout the Bible.

Shortly after Constantine became emperor, he moved the seat of the empire from Rome to a city in present-day Turkey that he named Constantinople. This became the city known as the capital of the Eastern Roman Empire, also called the Byzantine Empire. This lasted until the year 1453, when it was taken over by Islam. By this time, the seat of the empire had moved back to Rome; it had become once again the political center of the empire as well as its religious center since the days of Charlemagne around the year AD 800, when he was crowned by the existing pope as emperor of the Holy Roman Empire. This Holy Roman Empire, ruled by the Roman Catholic system, would go on to prosper through the collection of taxes, stealing property, persecution, conquest, etc. The pope, being the head of the religion and influencing the political climate, was very corrupt; religious terror throughout the empire kept its population spiritually ignorant and terrorized the poor under this so-called Roman Catholic Church. This made the institution one of the wealthiest, if not the wealthiest, in the world, wielding their religious and governmental power and influence over humanity, which gladly accepts it under the name of religion.

The list of their violent history, as mentioned before, includes forced conversions, forcing the Latin Bible on its subjects, and incorporating superstitious and pagan beliefs; nothing was rejected just so that the subjects would conform to their system. Under the Roman Empire, Jews were persecuted, thrown out of countries, and were easy prey for expulsion, exploitation, or death via a system devised by the Roman Empire called the Inquisition. Before that, the world had suffered the excesses of the Crusades sponsored by the Roman system, which inflicted terror on the people from Rome to Jerusalem. During the conquest of the Americas, the conquered were never evangelized; however, they were forced to convert, again incorporating their pagan practices into the Roman system, which, by the way, continues to this day. All that was required for conversion was that they would accept the Roman baptism.

CHAPTER 3

Delusion

Constantine had encouraged Jewish persecution since the time of his so-called conversion. He stated in a letter that Easter and Passover had to be separated by stating, "It appeared an unworthy thing that in the celebration of this most holy feast that we should follow the practice of the Jews who have impiously defiled their hands with enormous sin and are therefore afflicted with blindness of soul. Let us have nothing in common with that Jewish crowd because their hands have been stained with crime, the minds of these wretched men are necessary blinded. Let us then having nothing in common with the Jews who are our adversaries; let us avoid all contact with that evil way for we have received from our savior a different way. Therefore, their irregularity must be corrected in order that we may no more have nothing in common with those patricides and the murderers of our Lord."

In the year AD 329, he issued laws prohibiting Jews from owning Christian slaves and prohibiting mixed marriages between Christians and Jews. The long history of apostate teachings started its long descent into what we have now as official Roman Catholic doctrine. From the time Constantine made Christianity legal in the Empire to the present religious and political rule of the pope in the Roman Catholic system, this system has reigned supreme in delusion after the true religion of Christ. The current pope, Pope Francis, has been quoted saying about Mary, the mother of Jesus, that she is the great mother of God Most Holy, terrible as an army set in Array, and Saint Michael the Archangel, patron of the holy church and Prince of the Heavenly Host, will help all of us. Strong delusion.

By the time of Constantine's conversion, the Word of God was a finished product with clear warnings not to add to it or diminish from it; this warning was clearly ignored. Doctrine was what the Roman system desired and taught their subjects. False teachings emanated from his leaders, who accepted them as being equal or superior to the Word of God. And the Roman subjects would live under the threat of death if they should depart from their doctrine.

The Roman system instituted customs and traditions foreign to the true teachings of Christ. The Roman system established a system of sacraments as official church doctrine that leads to salvation. They would start the practice of calling their priest father, a clear contradiction to Jesus's teaching of calling no one father on earth because we have our Father in heaven. They would prefer infant baptism instead of baptism by immersion, prayers for the dead were accepted, and the doctrines of purgatory and Mariology were accepted in clear contradiction to established scripture. This system was steeped in a delusion which led to these traditions being on an equal basis with or superior to the Word of God. As the office of the pope would become institutionalized, they came to be known as God on earth, this being not much of a departure from the Roman emperors being worshiped as God. They do believe that the pope is Jesus on earth. Clear delusion.

Further addition to the list of abuses of this religious system is the fact that the seat of this system, the Vatican, is a country with a head of state as well as the head of the church called the Roman Catholic system. This confusion gives them the opportunity of never being clear whether they speak as a state or a church. This tactic further provides the opportunity of delusion by confusing and keeping them in a state of ignorance regarding their purpose. Remember that only until recent times were their official church services conducted in the Latin language, which people did not understand, keeping them ignorant of the scriptures.

The Roman Catholic system has been complicit in the persecution of Jews from before the time of Constantine through his rule into the time of the Crusades and the Inquisition, which included the official expulsion of the Jews from Spain in the year 1492. During Hitler's World War II, the Jews were almost eliminated. During the Holocaust, the Catholic system did not provide much resistance.

CHAPTER 4

Corruption

The Apostle Paul said in Scripture that we are not like those that corrupt the Word of God, as we have seen in the previous chapters that declare total corruption in the Roman Catholic system. The worst thing that ever happened to the world was the so-called conversion of Constantine, the emperor of Rome, to Christianity. We have also seen why this so-called conversion is in doubt regarding his behavior as a so-called Christian given his abuses, persecution, and lack of evidence regarding true Christian behavior. Instead, Constantine, in his subtle and devious ways, attempted to put out the light that Jesus had brought to the world. However, God made sure that His message remained in the pages of scripture that survived Constantine.

As God's message spread in spite of the Roman system, copies of scripture remained in the hands of the people. A lot of these scriptures had remained from the time of the Roman and later Byzantine Empire in the city of Constantinople and in different cities where people had made the effort to collect them. This precious collection of manuscripts had been largely ignored for their value as they had been replaced by Constantine's accepted Bible translated by Jerome, who used the translation of Eusebius. This was the only copy of the Bible that the Roman system ever used; only their officials had access to this Bible, not the general population. When Constantinople fell to the Muslims, the people fled to the rest of Europe with these treasured manuscripts. This transfer of knowledge into Europe coincided with a time in history known as the Renaissance. In this age and coming from the Dark Ages, people started questioning religious systems. While examining these new manuscripts absent for many years from the population, the readers, most of them within the Roman Catholic system, began to question the very teachings of this system.

The confusion, the persecutions, and the delusions perpetrated by this system, resulting in its utter corruption, became very evident. Some within set out to transform the system. Foremost in their minds, it became evident that salvation of the soul was available to humanity outside the system solely through the reading of scripture. This thirst for knowledge would question the very essence of what had occurred during those long, dark ages. Even before the fall of Constantinople, certain scholars had translated what was the Roman system Bible into their local languages, and in so doing, they discovered the treasures available through scripture about salvation. An example of such an individual was a man by the name of Wycliffe, who, while searching through the scripture, came to the realization that the scripture was meant to be read by everyone in their local language. In the flood of scripture available from Constantinople into Europe, people began to doubt what they had been taught by the Roman Catholic system.

I would remind the reader of the partial list of all teachings propagated by the Roman system; it became obvious that this has been a result of their fabrication and contrary to the teaching of scripture. Another such person was a man named Martin Luther, who was a priest of the Roman Catholic system; this man provided a much longer list of Roman Catholic teachings contrary to scripture.

There was a brilliant scholar named Erasmus who took advantage of those Greek language manuscripts that had arrived from Constantinople, and in light of the fact that the printing press had been invented, he printed the corrected Latin version based on the available Greek manuscripts that had just arrived in Europe from Constantinople. I would add that the previously mentioned Martin Luther took advantage of Erasmus's work to come to his conclusions.

Erasmus took those Greek language manuscripts that had just arrived from the Byzantine Empire, translated them into Latin, and compared his translation to the Roman Catholic Bible, which had been translated into Latin by Jerome in the fourth century from Eusebius's earlier Greek translation as commissioned by Constantine earlier in the same century. Erasmus concluded from his work that not only Constantine's doubtful conversion, the source of his Bible translation, and also Constantine's brand of Christianity differed substantially from what was intended.

Constantine's efforts only added to the darkness of the Dark Ages, the Middle Ages, and the Renaissance. Do not forget that this Renaissance age also included the age of the Inquisition. The Inquisition was instrumental in opposing much of what the Renaissance had to offer, especially in the area of religion. The battle for the uncorrupted Word of God had continued from the time of Christ through the time of the apostles, into the time of the early church fathers, through the time of Constantine, into the Dark Ages, through the Middle Ages, and finally to the Renaissance. The purity of God's teachings has never ceased. We saw the early Christians in Antioch, in Italy, in the Gothic regions, and without doubt in many other parts of the world that the Word of God had persevered in spite of severe persecution and bloodshed on the part of the Roman Catholic system. These abuses had not occurred in a vacuum; the very same priests within the system faced with this new knowledge and, with the arrival of the Renaissance, discovered that there was an alternative and the people's souls were at stake.

One such early church father outside the Roman system was a man called Irenaeus of the city of Lyon in the area of what is now France. He wrote a book titled *Against Heresies* in the year AD 180. Another such man was Polycarp, who, before he was martyred by the Roman Empire, wrote a letter called the "Epistle of Polycarp to the Philippians" in the second century AD. There was also Ignatius of Antioch; we remember that this is the city in Syria where Christians were first called "Christians," also of the second century after Christ. The list is long of early Bible-believing fathers who contended for the purity of the word and battled against heresies.

These early church fathers and many more like them continued to hold the faith through the Dark Ages, through the Middle Ages, and into the Renaissance. With the invention of the printing press, scriptures dating back many centuries shed their light again in the minds of the people as scripture became more available in the people's local languages.

CHAPTER 5

Destruction
The Roman Catholic System Civil War

The destruction of the Roman Catholic system started with the Roman Catholic Civil War, known as the Protestant Reformation, which started after the Bible was translated into local languages and produced in large quantities as a result of the invention of the printing press. The Roman Catholic system had been unable to stamp out Bible Christianity, but in spite of all their efforts throughout the centuries, true Bible Christianity continued from the time of Christ. The Bible declares that the church will be built and that the gates of hell will not prevail against it. Throughout history, after the time of Christ, groups of Bible believers, true Christians, such as the Albigenses and the Waldenses, among others, had the truth as preached by Christ, the apostles, and the church fathers, such as the ones mentioned in a previous chapter. All this in spite of the Roman system's attempt to stamp out Bible Christianity. These people had remained a true testimony to Bible Christianity; their testimony was their lives consecrated to Christ, preaching, salvation by grace, baptism by immersion, and signing with their blood, spilled by continued persecution from the time of the Roman Empire through the time of the Roman Catholic system instituted by Constantine.

The world had not been in total ignorance of true Bible teaching in spite of the Roman Catholic system persecuting and killing believers in their persecution. As the availability of Bible translations in people's local languages increased, the numbers of people turning away from the Roman system increased, which caused the Roman Catholic system to increase their persecution. The Jesuits came into existence for such a purpose: to infiltrate any movement that would be a threat to the system, using any method necessary to counter the "civil war." As more and more of their own priestly system read the scriptures, they would turn on the system, including men such as the aforementioned Luther Martin, and there were more to follow. The final result of this "civil war" was the formation of other systems that were Protestant in nature because they protested. Out of these protests came what we have come to know today as other religious denominations such as the Methodists, Presbyterians, Lutherans, and others, most of them retaining the trappings of the traditions and ritualistic forms of worship that had been established by the Roman Catholic system; others broke with some of the traditions while keeping some of the trappings of the old system. True Bible-believing Christians were never a part of this movement; they would continue to stand alone in true Bible Christianity. The Roman Catholic civil war was a success in the sense that it brought to light the false teachings of the system.

Those Bible-believing Christians who never had to revolt continue to this day, keeping their conversation, behavior, and beliefs true to what the early Christian fathers, apostles, and Christ himself taught. As we see, the Jesuit assault on this Protestant Reformation was not successful, even though they continue to this day to oppose the Reformation. The Roman Catholic system has modified from opposition in favor of reunification; the real Bible-believing Christians will never accept such an effort, just as their forefathers have done throughout the centuries, paying with their blood, with their freedom, and with their possessions their opposition to the Catholic system. Bible-believing Christians have remained faithful even in the face of persecution and death. Bible-believing Christians were the testimony necessary for the Roman Catholic civil war to occur. The Roman system tried to win the civil war, in which they failed and tried accommodations with the Reformation (civil war), which has not been totally successful, but in an effort to stamp out

Bible Christianity, they tried another approach: attacking the true source of Bible Christianity, the Bible itself. The great result of the Catholic civil war was the creation of the King James Bible. This Bible is the result of those earlier Bibles by early Bible-believing Christians, together with those treasured manuscripts that had been stored centuries earlier in Constantinople. The creation of the King James Bible went to the heart of the Roman Catholic system, which depended on its unique Bible for many centuries. Now they needed to discredit the King James Bible. Their approach was to come up with new translations that have produced hundreds of Bibles that pervert the Word of God. Not much has changed since the conversion of Constantine the emperor.

CHAPTER 6

Purification
The Purity of the Word, Psalm 12:6, Proverbs 9:1

In chapter 5, we saw how true Bible-believing Christians maintained their beliefs preserved in those Greek manuscripts coming from Constantinople. As these were translated into English, German, and other European languages, people discovered the treasures contained in the Word of God that had been hidden from the people by the Roman Catholic system through the previous centuries. It will take a completely different book to detail the intricacies of the political and religious influence that the explosion of Bibles produced. Suffice it to say that with the many more Bibles available, the people's access to them increased, and new believers were added daily, just as in the days of the apostles.

Bible translations continued to proliferate, especially in the English language, such as the Tyndale Bible, the Cloverdale Bible, the Geneva Bible, the Great Bible, and the Bishops Bible, to name a few. There were Bibles in the German language, French, Spanish, Italian, and other languages. The work that Erasmus produced and the availability of the printing press had become the spark that started the Catholic civil war. Erasmus's work had become the basis for a translation that would challenge the existing Catholic system Bible available for many centuries. In England, the official English church preferred the use of the Bishop's Bible, while the Puritans preferred the use of the Geneva Bible. When King James of Scotland became king of England, he became aware of the need to have a common Bible for the kingdom. He managed to get both parties to agree to the production of a new Bible in the year 1604, and a commission was formed to produce a new Bible translation. Brilliant men from the appropriate fields of discipline were chosen; fifty-four started the project, and forty-seven finished it in the year 1611. The final product came to be known as the Authorized Version of the Bible, and today, we know it as the King James Bible of 1611.

This Bible became the most used in the English-speaking world until the middle of the nineteenth century, when new Bible translations began to be produced from a different source of manuscripts that had not been used to produce the King James Bible. In a short time, the English-speaking world would reach around the world. It was said that it was the empire where the sun never set that the world would come to know for the first time because of the King James Bible about Jesus Christ and his gospel, not the gospel of the Roman Catholic system. The Roman Catholic system would sit in stark contrast to the gospel of the King James Bible. The Roman Catholic system would forcibly convert its subjects through threats of death and persecution, whether economic or physical.

The English-speaking world, through the influence of the King James Bible, would produce countries such as the United States of America, which was largely influenced by its teachings. Wherever the English language went, through the influence of the King James Bible and true Bible-believing Christians, such as in the country of India, as soon as they could, they would start the good works of building orphanages, hospitals, and churches that would promote the gospel. The King James Bible would promote salvation by faith and make it known throughout the world. These are just examples of the difference it makes when a ruling people has the King James Bible as a guide versus the Roman Catholic system, which only had monetary gains to obtain from their conquests.

To quote Pastor Jared Longsine in a message called "Seven Reasons to Read the King James Bible," he says, "The Bible that is in the hands of most, if not all, people here today come from a rich history. It is an accurate translation. This Bible has changed the complexion of the world. It gave the ordinary man access to an extraordinary God."

CHAPTER 7

Preservation

Regarding the King James Bible translation, I will quote from the book *The King James Version: By Inspiration or Translation* by author J Paul Reno. He says, quoting from the King James Bible translators view of their task, "These men were chosen for their superior linguistic skills. They used those skills in careful examination of the Hebrew, Aramaic, and Greek texts. They compared the previous English translations. They consulted the translation work of Bibles in other languages. These commendable actions were proper for translation. They took what was available and revised, revised, and revised. This is not the process of inspiration but of a great translation…they did that because of who they were…translators."

The Roman Catholic system came up with ways to discredit, attack, and subvert the great success and impact on humanity of the availability of the King James Bible. To this day, the King James Bible appears on their list of prohibited books. Their only alternative was the official Roman Catholic system's Latin Vulgate Bible, which was not available to the common person. Their worship services were in Latin, and the reading of the scriptures was in the Latin of their Bible, subject to the interpretation of scripture exclusively by the Roman officers of the Catholic system called priests. The Roman Catholic system, after seeing their religious and political influence diminished by the power of scripture as available through the King James Bible, developed a different tactic. They would attack the creators of the King James Bible and attack, attack, and attack until, in the middle of the 19th century, sympathizers of the Roman Catholic system and enemies of the King James Bible came up with a new tactic: create a new translation that would differ from the King James Bible, therefore subverting the pure teaching of Christ with the elimination of key passages, words, etc. These new translations have been accomplished by people and organizations that don't believe that Jesus is God, that don't believe he was born of a virgin, that salvation is by faith alone, that don't believe in the soon return of Christ, etc. Can you really trust these translations when compared to the purity of the King James Bible, whose roots can be traced back to the time of the apostles?

The Roman Catholic system, being such "masters of confusion," continues to influence the world's population by speaking out of both sides of their mouth, on one side from their political nature and on the other side from their religious nature. The unfortunate members of this system continue in their ignorance since they are not encouraged to seek Jesus on a personal basis but only through engagement in the ritualistic system. My only aim is to highlight the fact that when Christianity is mentioned, it is not reflected by the image of a person wearing a turned-around collar, but that true Christianity is reflected by those people who were first called Christians in Antioch.

REFERENCE LIST

The material for this work was derived from several sources. Apologies to the ones that I may not have listed below. Thanks all for your contribution.

biblestudytools.com. "Bible Versions and Translations Online."
"Christian History Timeline: How We Got Our Bible"
Christianity in View. "Timeline of Christian History"
Dynamicatholic.com. "A Guide to 10 Popular Marian Apparitions."
Gill Books. "Martin Luther and the Reformation."
GotQuestions.org.
historic-uk.com. "The King James Bible."
Hoggard, Pastor M. Prophetic Research Ministries. Festus, Missouri.
Jones, F. N. *Which Version Is the Bible 21st Edition*. King World Press
King James Bible
King James Bible Research Council conference materials
King James Bible translators letter to the readers
Maryourhelp.org. "Introduction to Mariology."
mycatholiclife.org. "Catholic Saints A-Z."
Odom, Pastor T. First Baptist Church of Southwest Broward.
Pastor James Knox sermon series on the KJV. Bible Baptist Church.
    DeLand, Florida.
pewresearch.org. "Protestantism."
Pinto, C. J. Adullam films
scholar.library.miami.edu. "Afrocuban Religion and Syncretism with
    the Catholic Religion." University of Miami Digital Collections.
thecripplegate.com. "5 Differences Between Catholic Theology and
    the Gospel."
Wikipedia. "Queen Of Heaven," "Constantine the Great," "Spanish
    Inquisition," "Crusades."

ABOUT THE AUTHOR

Alejandro Amores is a husband, son, father, and grandfather. He was a sinner saved by grace and is now a servant of the Lord. His life verse is Joshua 24:15: "And if it seem evil unto you to serve the Lord, choose you this day whom ye will serve; whether the gods which your fathers served that were on the other side of the flood, or the gods of the Amorites, in whose land ye dwell: but as for me and my house, we will serve the Lord." Amores is dedicated to Christianity and a defender of the King James Version.

www.ingramcontent.com/pod-product-compliance
Lightning Source LLC
Chambersburg PA
CBHW031639170726
47990CB00018B/1554